WNBA SUPERSTARS
CANDACE PARKER
by Heather Rule

WWW.FOCUSREADERS.COM

Copyright © 2022 by Focus Readers®, Lake Elmo, MN 55042. All rights reserved. No part of this book may be reproduced or utilized in any form or by any means without written permission from the publisher.

Focus Readers is distributed by North Star Editions:
sales@northstareditions.com | 888-417-0195

Produced for Focus Readers by Red Line Editorial.

Photographs ©: Jordon Kelly/Cal Sport Media/AP Images, cover, 1; Jim Mone/AP Images, 4–5, 6, 9; Ty Russell/The Oklahoman/AP Images, 10–11; Wade Payne/AP Images, 13; Amy Sancetta/AP Images, 15; Gus Ruelas/AP Images, 16–17; Stacy Bengs/AP Images, 18; Elaine Thompson/AP Images, 21; Ringo H. W. Chiu/AP Images, 22–23; Jae C. Hong/AP Images, 24; Chris O'Meara/AP Images, 27; Eileen T. Meslar/AP Images, 28

Library of Congress Cataloging-in-Publication Data
Names: Rule, Heather, author.
Title: Candace Parker / by Heather Rule.
Description: Lake Elmo, MN : Focus Readers, 2022. | Series: WNBA superstars | Includes index. | Audience: Grades 4-6
Identifiers: LCCN 2021041137 (print) | LCCN 2021041138 (ebook) | ISBN 9781637390696 (hardcover) | ISBN 9781637391235 (paperback) | ISBN 9781637391778 (ebook) | ISBN 9781637392256 (pdf)
Subjects: LCSH: Parker, Candace, 1986---Juvenile literature. | Women basketball players--United States--Biography--Juvenile literature.
Classification: LCC GV884.P36 R85 2022 (print) | LCC GV884.P36 (ebook) | DDC 796.323092 [B]--dc23
LC record available at https://lccn.loc.gov/2021041137
LC ebook record available at https://lccn.loc.gov/2021041138

Printed in the United States of America
Mankato, MN
012022

ABOUT THE AUTHOR
Heather Rule is a freelance sports journalist, author, and social media coordinator. She has a bachelor's degree in journalism and mass communication from the University of St. Thomas.

TABLE OF CONTENTS

CHAPTER 1
Ending on a High Note 5

CHAPTER 2
First to Dunk 11

CHAPTER 3
On Fire with the Sparks 17

PAVING THE WAY
Tina Thompson 21

CHAPTER 4
Long Way Home 23

At a Glance • 29
Focus on Candace Parker • 30
Glossary • 31
To Learn More • 32
Index • 32

CHAPTER 1
ENDING ON A HIGH NOTE

The 2016 Women's National Basketball Association (WNBA) Finals came down to a one-point game. Candace Parker and the Los Angeles Sparks trailed the Minnesota Lynx 74–73 in Game 5. The Sparks had the ball with just 23 seconds to go. Sparks forward Nneka Ogwumike passed the ball to Parker in the lane.

Candace Parker puts up a shot during Game 5 of the 2016 WNBA Finals between the Los Angeles Sparks and the Minnesota Lynx.

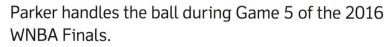
Parker handles the ball during Game 5 of the 2016 WNBA Finals.

Parker quickly shot the ball into the basket. The Sparks now led by one point.

However, the Lynx took back the lead with 15 seconds on the clock. Sparks guard Chelsea Gray dribbled the ball downcourt. She missed a fadeaway jumper. But Ogwumike grabbed the rebound. With three seconds left, Ogwumike sank the go-ahead shot. Then the final buzzer sounded. The Sparks were WNBA champions. And Parker had led the way with a game-high 28 points and 12 rebounds. In her ninth season in the league, Parker finally had a WNBA title.

Sparks players jumped around in celebration. Parker hugged teammate Kristi Toliver with one hand. Parker held the game ball with the other. And she didn't let go of it. She held the ball for interviews. She held it when she was named the Finals Most Valuable Player (MVP). Parker's eyes were filled with tears when she talked to a TV reporter. Parker pointed to the ball in her hand. She said the championship was for Pat.

Parker was talking about Pat Summitt. Summitt had coached Parker in college. She had died earlier that year. Before

MENTOR AT TENNESSEE

Pat Summitt coached the University of Tennessee's Lady Vols for 38 years. She helped make the women's basketball team one of the best in the United States. Summitt won 1,098 games and eight national titles there. When she died in 2016, no other college basketball coach, male or female, had won as many games.

Parker (right) celebrates after winning the 2016 WNBA Finals.

Game 5, Parker had listened to one of Summitt's speeches. Losing Summitt was one of many tough parts of the year for Parker. But becoming a WNBA champion helped end the year on a high note.

CHAPTER 2

FIRST TO DUNK

Candace Parker was born on April 19, 1986. She grew up in Naperville, Illinois. Candace quickly fell in love with basketball. She started playing on teams at age six. In high school, Candace became a national star. During her second year, she became the first girl in Illinois to dunk in a basketball game.

Candace Parker won the slam-dunk contest at the 2004 All American high school game.

Then, in 2003, she led her high school team to a state championship. She led them to a second straight title in 2004.

Parker began attending the University of Tennessee in the fall of 2004. But she was struggling with a knee injury. So, she decided to be a **redshirt** her first year. By the 2005–06 season, Parker had added 3 inches (8 cm) to her vertical leap. The extra air paid off. That season, Parker dunked twice in a National Collegiate Athletic Association (NCAA) tournament game. No woman had ever dunked twice in an NCAA game before.

Parker took the whole team to great heights in 2006–07. She led the Lady

Parker dunks during a 2006 game with the University of Tennessee.

Vols to a 34–3 record that season. Tennessee made it all the way to the NCAA championship. During the title game, Parker was double- and triple-teamed by the Rutgers defense.

But she still scored 17 points. She also muscled in the paint to grab seven rebounds. Parker and the Lady Vols ended up winning 59–46. It was the team's first national championship in nine years.

A year later, Parker and Tennessee were back in the national title game. This time, the Lady Vols beat Stanford 64–48 for back-to-back NCAA titles. Parker recorded 17 points and nine rebounds in the game. In both 2007 and 2008, Parker was named the Final Four Most Outstanding Player. She became only the fourth player to receive the honor twice.

Parker's career at Tennessee was one of the best ever. She was the school's third

Parker soars for a shot during the 2008 NCAA championship.

all-time leading scorer with 2,137 points. She was also the school's record holder with 275 blocks. Parker could have played another year at Tennessee. But she had her sights on the next level. Parker was headed to the WNBA.

CHAPTER 3

ON FIRE WITH THE SPARKS

Candace Parker was a superstar from the start. The Los Angeles Sparks selected her in the 2008 WNBA **draft**. She was the No. 1 overall pick. Parker lived up to the hype. Her first game was the greatest **debut** in WNBA history. She recorded 34 points, 12 rebounds, eight **assists**, two steals, and a block.

Candace Parker drives to the basket during her first WNBA season in 2008.

Parker drives past a Minnesota Lynx defender during a 2012 game.

That first game showed why Parker was already one of the best. She could do everything on the court. She could score from the **low post** with amazing moves. She could shoot from mid-range and also hit threes. And her ball-handling skills let her drive past any defender. Parker brought out the best in her team, too. She knew when to pass to her teammates. Her rebounds and steals helped others score on fast breaks.

The 22-year-old kept up her incredible play all year. Parker became the first

A STAR AROUND THE WORLD

Parker's success wasn't limited to the WNBA. In both 2008 and 2012, she won an Olympic gold medal with Team USA. Parker also played in leagues overseas. That's partly because WNBA players earn low pay. So, they play in other leagues to earn extra money. Between 2010 and 2018, Parker played for teams in Russia, China, and Turkey. In 2013, she helped her Russian team win the EuroLeague championship.

WNBA player to win both **Rookie** of the Year and MVP in the same season.

Unfortunately for Sparks fans, Parker didn't play another full season for a few years. She took time off in 2009 after having her first child. Then she faced injuries in 2010 and 2011.

Parker was back in action in 2012. She started nearly every game and racked up 18 **double-doubles** in the season. She continued her All-Star play the next two years. Plus, the Sparks kept making the playoffs. But they got knocked out each year before the Finals. For years, Parker was one of the best players without a WNBA title.

PAVING THE WAY

TINA THOMPSON

Growing up, Candace Parker looked up to Tina Thompson. Thompson won four straight championships with the Houston Comets from 1997 to 2000. She won an Olympic gold medal with Team USA in both 2004 and 2008. Then, in 2009, she joined Parker in Los Angeles. Thompson and Parker were Sparks teammates for three seasons. Thompson finished her 17-year career with the Seattle Storm in 2013. When she retired, she was the WNBA's all-time leading scorer with 7,488 points.

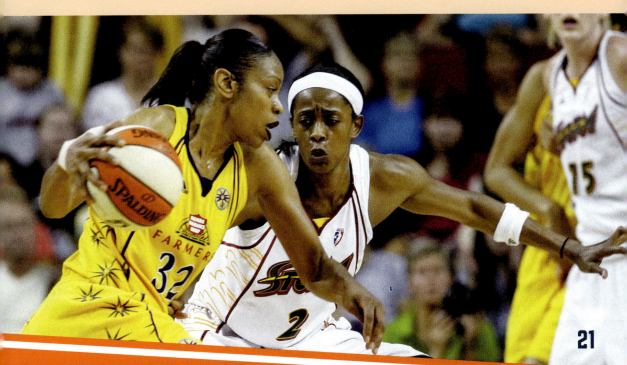

Tina Thompson (left) drives to the basket during a 2009 game with the Los Angeles Sparks.

CHAPTER 4

LONG WAY HOME

Los Angeles put it all together in 2016. Candace Parker and Nneka Ogwumike led the way. The pair balanced each other well. Parker provided sharp critical thinking. Ogwumike brought a strong positive attitude. Ogwumike earned regular-season MVP honors. Parker took the Finals MVP and her first WNBA title.

Candace Parker shoots a jumper during the 2016 WNBA semifinals against the Chicago Sky.

Parker blocks a New York Liberty player during a 2017 game.

The Sparks looked for a repeat in 2017. They finished with the same 26–8 record as in their 2016 season. And the WNBA Finals were a rematch against the Minnesota Lynx. The Sparks got one win away from back-to-back championships. But they couldn't seal the deal. The Lynx won the next two games to take the title.

Parker played another great season in 2018. She reached her fifth WNBA All-Star Game. She averaged nearly 18 points per game. However, the Sparks weren't as strong overall. They fell short in the playoffs.

Things went further downhill for Parker in 2019. She faced more injuries and missed 12 games. When she could play, her game struggled. She hit career-low numbers on both offense and defense. Los Angeles ended up being swept in the semifinals by the Connecticut Sun.

Some basketball experts thought Parker was nearing the end of her WNBA career. She'd faced injury after injury. And going into 2020, Parker was 34 years old. But Parker wasn't done. To prepare for the season, she worked out more than ever.

Her efforts paid off. In 2020, Parker led the WNBA with 9.7 rebounds per

BEYOND THE GAME

Parker works hard on and off the court. In 2018, she became the only full-time female NBA **analyst** for Turner Sports. Parker also supports efforts to find cures for **Alzheimer's disease**. This illness affected Parker's college coach, Pat Summitt. Parker works to help address children's hunger, too. And she proudly speaks out on social justice issues.

Parker steals the ball from a Liberty player during a 2020 game.

game. She was one of only five players to average at least one block and one steal per game. She was named the 2020 Defensive Player of the Year. Parker proved she still had a lot of talent left.

The 2020 season was Parker's 13th for the Los Angeles Sparks. She decided she

Parker prepares to shoot a three-pointer during a 2021 game with the Chicago Sky.

wanted a change. So, in 2021, she signed with the Chicago Sky. It proved to be a great decision. In 2021, Parker helped the Sky make it all the way to the Finals. In Game 4, Parker scored 16 points and pulled down 13 rebounds. The Sky won the game and the series. For the second time in her career, Parker was a WNBA champion!

AT A GLANCE

CANDACE PARKER

- Height: 6 feet 4 inches (193 cm)
- Weight: 175 pounds (79 kg)
- Birth date: April 19, 1986
- Birthplace: St. Louis, Missouri
- High school: Naperville Central High School (Naperville, Illinois)
- College: University of Tennessee (Knoxville, Tennessee) (2004–2008)
- Pro teams: Los Angeles Sparks (2008–2020); Chicago Sky (2021–)
- Major awards: Olympic gold medal (2008, 2012); WNBA Rookie of the Year (2008); WNBA MVP (2008, 2013); WNBA All-Star (2011, 2013–2014, 2017–2018, 2021); WNBA champion (2016, 2021); WNBA Finals MVP (2016); WNBA Defensive Player of the Year (2020)

FOCUS ON
CANDACE PARKER

Write your answers on a separate piece of paper.

1. Write a letter to a friend explaining what you learned about Candace Parker and her mentor, Pat Summitt.

2. Would you want to model your basketball game after Parker's? Why or why not?

3. When did Parker win the Defensive Player of the Year award?

    A. 2008
    B. 2016
    C. 2020

4. Why did Parker's dunks in high school and college get her so much attention?

    A. Few female basketball players had dunked in games before then.
    B. No basketball players have dunked since then.
    C. Parker was one of many female basketball players to dunk.

Answer key on page 32.

GLOSSARY

Alzheimer's disease
A disease that causes the brain to break down, often leading to problems with memory and thinking.

analyst
A person who explains details about a certain topic.

assists
Passes that lead directly to a teammate scoring.

debut
First appearance.

double-doubles
Games in which a player has double-digit numbers in two categories.

draft
A system that allows teams to acquire new players coming into a league.

low post
The area near the basket on a basketball court.

redshirt
A member of a college team who can practice with the team but can't play in games.

rookie
A professional athlete in his or her first year.

TO LEARN MORE

BOOKS

Buckey, A. W. *Women in Basketball*. Lake Elmo, MN: Focus Readers, 2020.

Frederick, Shane. *Candace Parker: Basketball Star*. North Mankato, MN: Capstone Press, 2020.

Omoth, Tyler. *The WNBA Finals*. North Mankato, MN: Capstone Press, 2020.

NOTE TO EDUCATORS

Visit **www.focusreaders.com** to find lesson plans, activities, links, and other resources related to this title.

INDEX

All-Star, 20, 25

Chicago Sky, 28

Connecticut Sun, 25

Defensive Player of the Year, 27

EuroLeague championship, 19

Gray, Chelsea, 6

Los Angeles Sparks, 5–7, 17, 20, 21, 23–25, 27

Minnesota Lynx, 5–6, 24–25

Most Valuable Player (MVP), 7, 20, 23

Naperville, Illinois, 11

National Collegiate Athletic Association (NCAA), 12–14

Ogwumike, Nneka, 5–7, 23

Olympics, 19, 21

Rookie of the Year, 20

Summit, Pat, 8–9, 26

Thompson, Tina, 21

Toliver, Kristi, 7

University of Tennessee, 8, 12–15

WNBA Finals, 5, 7, 20, 23–24, 28

Answer Key: 1. Answers will vary; 2. Answers will vary; 3. C; 4. A